COMPLEX PTSD, TRAUMA AND RECOVERY

A PRACTICAL GUIDE TO OVERCOME TRAUMATIC
EVENTS AND LIVE A PEACEFUL LIFE. ENHANCE YOUR
MOOD AND BOOST YOUR CREATIVITY FROM NOW

REINER HARTMANN

D1692390

REINER HARTMANN PRESS

WHY THIS BOOK

Thank you for giving this book on complex post-traumatic stress disorder (C-PTSD), trauma, and recovery a chance. We understand that the journey towards healing from trauma can be a challenging one, but we hope that this book will provide you with the knowledge, insights, and tools you need to navigate that journey.

One of the things that sets this book apart from others on the topic is its comprehensive approach. We cover a wide range of topics related to C-PTSD, including its definition, symptoms, causes, and triggers. We also delve into the topic of trauma more broadly, discussing its definition, causes, and impact on mental health. And, of course, we provide detailed information on the diagnosis and treatment of C-PTSD, as well as self-help tips and strategies for managing the condition.

In addition, this book includes two bonus chapters on the power of living in the present and how to identify and manage emotional pain. These chapters offer valuable insights and practical strategies that can help you to better cope with the challenges of C-PTSD and the aftermath of trauma.

As you read this book, we encourage you to take your time and absorb the information at your own pace. Remember that recovery is a process, and it is important to be patient and kind to yourself. If at any point you feel overwhelmed or uncertain, please don't hesitate to reach out to a trusted friend, family member, or mental health professional for support.

At the end of this book, we would greatly appreciate it if you could take a few minutes to leave a review.

Your feedback helps us to understand what you found most helpful and valuable in the book, and it also helps other readers to make informed decisions about whether this book is right for them. Additionally, we invite you to send a selfie to reviewcustomer@reinerhart mannpress.com or to publish a photo review on the channel where you purchased this book.

We would love to see your journey of recovery and hear your thoughts about this book.

We hope that you find this book to be a valuable resource on your path towards healing and hope.

Remember that you are not alone and that there is hope for a brighter future.

CONTENTS

BONUS CHAPTER 1

BONUS CHAPTER 2

HOW TO READ THIS BOOK

Here are some additional tips for reading a book on complex post-traumatic stress disorder (PTSD), trauma, and recovery:

1. **Set goals for your reading**. Consider what you hope to gain from reading the book and how much time you want to devote to reading each day or week. Having clear goals can help you stay focused and motivated.
2. **Keep a journal**. Writing about your thoughts and feelings as you read can be a helpful way to process the material and reflect on your own experiences.
3. **Take breaks and practice self-care.** As mentioned before, reading about complex PTSD and trauma can be emotionally taxing. Make sure to take breaks and practice self-care while reading. This might include activities such as going for a walk, talking to a trusted friend or family member, or engaging in a hobby you enjoy.
4. **Consider seeking support from a mental health professional**. If you find that reading about complex PTSD and trauma is triggering for you, or if you are struggling

with your own experiences of trauma, it may be helpful to speak with a mental health professional. They can provide support and guidance as you work through the material.

5. **Don't feel like you have to rush through the book**. It's important to take the time you need to process the material and integrate it into your understanding of complex PTSD and trauma.

6. **Reflect on what you have learned**. After you have finished reading the book, take some time to reflect on what you have learned and how it may be relevant to your own experiences or the experiences of others you know.

Overall, the key is to approach the material at a pace that feels comfortable and manageable for you. Remember to take breaks and practice self-care, and seek additional support if needed.

HERE IS A MORE DETAILED SUMMARY OF WHAT YOU CAN EXPECT TO FIND IN EACH CHAPTER OF THIS BOOK:

Chapter 1: COMPLEX PTSD

- **Definition and explanation of complex PTSD**: This chapter provides an in-depth explanation of what complex PTSD is and how it differs from other types of PTSD.
- **Symptoms of complex PTSD**: This chapter lists and describes the various symptoms of complex PTSD, such as intense emotional reactions, difficulty regulating emotions, and difficulty trusting others.
- **Causes of complex PTSD**: This chapter discusses the factors that can contribute to the development of complex PTSD, including prolonged or repeated exposure to traumatic events.

- **Triggers of complex PTSD**: This chapter explains what can trigger symptoms of complex PTSD and how to recognize and manage these triggers.
- **Coping behaviors of people with complex PTSD**: This chapter discusses the types of coping behaviors that people with complex PTSD may engage in, such as avoidance or substance abuse, and how to address these behaviors.

Chapter 2: PTSD

- **Definition and explanation of PTSD**: This chapter provides an overview of what PTSD is and how it is diagnosed.
- **How complex PTSD differs from PTSD**: This chapter explains the differences between complex PTSD and other types of PTSD, including the duration and severity of the traumatic events that lead to the development of the conditions.
- **Causes of PTSD**: This chapter discusses the types of events that can cause PTSD
- **Symptoms of PTSD**: This chapter lists and describes the various symptoms of PTSD, such as flashbacks, avoidance of triggers, and difficulty sleeping.
- **Management of PTSD**: This chapter discusses various treatment options for PTSD, such as cognitive-behavioral therapy and medication.

Chapter 3: TRAUMA

- **Definition and explanation of trauma**: This chapter provides a definition of trauma and explains how it can affect an individual's physical, emotional, and mental health.
- **Acute stress disorder**: This chapter discusses acute stress disorder, a condition that can occur after a traumatic event, and how it differs from PTSD.

- **Causes of trauma**: This chapter lists and describes the types of events that can cause trauma, such as physical or sexual abuse, accidents, and natural disasters.
- **Symptoms of trauma**: This chapter describes the physical, emotional, and behavioral symptoms that can result from trauma.
- **Trauma and the link to mental health**: This chapter discusses the relationship between trauma and mental health conditions, such as depression and anxiety.

Chapter 4: RECOVERING FROM COMPLEX PTSD: DIAGNOSIS AND TREATMENT

- **How the diagnosis of post-traumatic stress disorder is made**: This chapter explains the process of diagnosing complex PTSD, including the criteria that must be met and the types of assessments that may be used.
- **Treatment options for complex PTSD**: This chapter discusses the various treatment options for complex PTSD, including therapy, medication, and self-help strategies.
- **Self-help tips for individuals with complex PTSD**: This chapter provides practical tips for managing complex PTSD on a daily basis, such as setting boundaries, practicing self-care, and seeking support from loved ones.
- **How you can avoid exacerbating complex PTSD and its related complications**: This chapter discusses strategies for avoiding behaviors or situations that may worsen complex PTSD symptoms or lead to related complications.
- **How to avoid developing avoidance behaviors to cope with complex PTSD**: This chapter explains how avoidance behaviors can be a natural response to complex PTSD, but can ultimately be counterproductive in the long-term. It offers tips for replacing avoidance behaviors with more adaptive coping strategies.

- **How to live with C-PTSD and regain emotional control**: This chapter provides strategies for living with complex PTSD and regaining a sense of control over one's emotions. It discusses the importance of finding a balance between acknowledging and processing difficult emotions, while also setting limits on how much emotional energy one expends on them.

Bonus Chapter 1: THE POWER OF NOW

- **Living in the present**: This chapter discusses the benefits of living in the present moment and letting go of the past.
- **Letting go of the past**: This chapter offers tips for letting go of past events or experiences that may be causing distress.
- **How to live in the present**: This chapter provides practical tips for cultivating a present-moment focus, such as mindfulness practices and gratitude exercises.
- **Practice patience, even when it's hard**: This chapter discusses the benefits of practicing patience and offers strategies for developing this skill.

Bonus Chapter 2: HOW TO IDENTIFY AND MANAGE EMOTIONAL PAIN

- **How to identify and manage emotional pain**: This chapter provides an overview of how to recognize and manage emotional pain.
- **What causes emotional pain**: This chapter lists and describes the various causes of emotional pain, such as loss, rejection, and trauma.
- **Why does emotional pain feel physical**: This chapter explains the link between emotions and physical sensations and how emotional pain can manifest in physical ways.
- **Ways to manage emotional pain**: This chapter provides strategies for managing and coping with emotional pain,

such as seeking support from others, practicing self-care, and seeking professional help.

- **Your ego can blind you**: This chapter discusses the role of the ego in causing and prolonging emotional pain and offers strategies for managing the ego's influence.

ABOUT THE AUTHOR

Reiner Hartmann is a leading expert on the vagus nerve and the author of "Daily Vagus Nerve Exercises," a comprehensive guide to understanding and improving vagal tone. Born in 1967 in Bologna, Italy, Reiner has dedicated himself to learning about and sharing insights on the vagus nerve, a crucial part of the body's nervous system that plays a key role in physical and emotional well-being.

Through his writing, Reiner has helped thousands of readers around the world learn about the importance of the vagus nerve and how to take care of it. His book has been published worldwide, including on Amazon.com, and has received rave reviews from readers for its clear and concise information and practical exercises.

In his free time, Reiner enjoys staying active and exploring new interests. He is always seeking new opportunities to learn and grow, both personally and professionally. Whether through writing or other endeavors, Reiner is committed to helping others achieve optimal health and well-being.

INTRODUCTION

Trauma is a common experience for many people. In the past, trauma was thought of as a single event, like a car accident or a violent assault. But now we know that trauma can be caused by a number of factors. Things such as chronic stress, childhood abuse, and even a lack of social support all increase your chances of developing Post-Traumatic Stress Disorder (PTSD).

As a result of our wrong thinking, many people think that PTSD is the height of all trauma-related disorders. However, this is not exactly correct. While people who experience one traumatic event are likely to develop PTSD, people who experience multiple traumatic events are much more likely to develop complex PTSD.

Post-traumatic stress disorder (PTSD) is an anxiety disorder that can develop after experiencing a traumatic event, including in war zones and natural disasters. In these situations, people may feel extreme physical or emotional distress in response to the memories or reminders of their experience.

Complex PTSD describes when your symptoms are more than just those of PTSD; they also include other symptoms such as depression, anger, or substance abuse. This can happen when you experience multiple traumas at once or when you're exposed to other stressors that compound your symptoms.

Unfortunately, many people with this condition don't get diagnosed until they're already experiencing symptoms like panic attacks and extreme anxiety. Since you are reading this, however, it is safe to assume that you or someone you love has been diagnosed with PTSD.

In this book, we'll be discussing how trauma affects your body and mind, how it might affect your relationships with others, and how it might manifest itself physically in your body. We'll also discuss how you can cope with complex PTSD so that you can live well in spite of the constant presence of its symptoms.

This book is not only for those who have experienced trauma, but it's also for those who want to help others who have been affected by it. We will be discussing the similarities and differences between Complex PTSD and PTSD, the symptoms, effects, and most importantly, treatment of these conditions.

You will also find information about:

- How trauma affects your body and mind
- What causes trauma and how it affects your life
- How to take care of yourself during the healing process
- How to talk about your experiences without triggering yourself or others around you

It's going to be a long fulfilling ride, so put on your seatbelt and let's begin!

COMPLEX PTSD

*a*t one point in life, many individuals may have experienced a particularly traumatic event such as the death of a loved one, or a ghastly accident that overwhelmed all the coping mechanisms they have and altered their psychology and core personality. While not all of these events may result in post-traumatic disorder or complex PTSD, it does not take away from the fact that this is a debilitating condition suffered by many. Research shows that approximately 3% of the population in the United States may experience complex post-traumatic stress disorder.

Before discussing Complex PTSD, it would also be important to understand the science behind the development of this condition to give us a better understanding of the course, symptoms, and management of complex PTSD. The human body has several ways of handling stress and unpleasant situations. This is to prevent us from getting too overwhelmed by these events, which may eventually result in a crippling inability to live life normally. The major systems involved in this regulation are the sympathetic and parasympathetic divisions of the autonomic nervous system.

In stressful situations, the amygdala of the limbic system in the brain recognizes the presence of danger and prompts the sympathetic nervous system, also known as the "fight, freeze or flight" system to stimulate the release of stress hormones such as cortisol and adrenaline. These hormones then cause an increase in energy supply to the body as well as in heart rate and blood pressure to enable adequate blood flow throughout the body in preparation for the proper response.

They also increase glucose utilization by the body -especially the brain- and tone down bodily activities that may not be essential in such difficult situations. Once the harmful situation has passed, the parasympathetic division, also known as the "rest and digest" system kicks in to reset the body back to a calmer and more relaxed state. This helps you return to performing your normal activities with little or no drawbacks.

However, this is not the case in Complex PTSD as the balance between the divisions is removed. The amygdala, which is responsible for detecting danger, becomes overactive and this causes the hippocampus, which is responsible for the formation of long-term memory and recollection of events to be repressed. This eventually results in uncontrolled and devastating flashbacks of the event, especially when the individual encounters similar triggers, long after the initial event has passed. Ultimately, the body remains in a constant "fight, freeze or fight" mode and this is particularly responsible for the presentation and symptoms associated with complex PTSD.

WHAT IS COMPLEX PTSD?

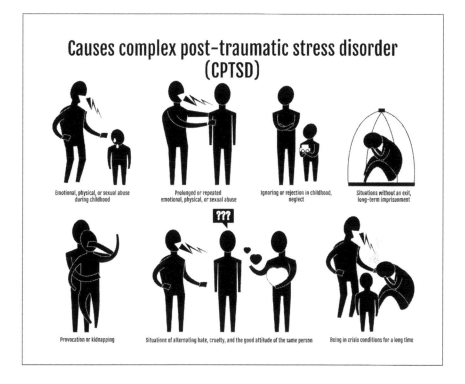

Complex Post Traumatic Stress Disorder (Complex PTSD), also referred to as complex trauma disorder is a psychological condition that ensues in an individual following the occurrence or exposure to a series of extreme, prolonged, or repeated traumatic incidents that last for months or years.

It was first described in 1992 by an American psychiatrist and scholar Judith Lewis Herman in her book titled *Trauma & Recovery*. For a long time, little was known about how to properly identify and diagnose Complex PTSD, however, it was recently added to the World Health Organization's eleventh revision of the International Classification of Diseases and Related Health Problems (ICD-11).

The symptoms of Complex PTSD are similar to those of Post Traumatic Stress Disorder (PTSD). However, unlike PTSD, which is caused by a single traumatic event in a person's life, Complex PTSD is caused by repeated exposure to trauma from multiple sources. The effects of this exposure can last for decades after the initial trauma has occurred.

Complex PTSD is characterized by symptoms such as flashbacks (a sudden recollection of an event), chronic anxiety, depression, and difficulty sleeping. Complex PTSD sufferers may also experience nightmares about being attacked in the same fashion as during the traumatic incident. In addition to these symptoms, Complex PTSD sufferers are prone to experiencing irritability and anger outbursts when confronted with reminders of their traumatic experiences.

These symptoms can cause extreme distress in those who suffer from Complex PTSD because they feel as though they are reliving their trauma over and over again throughout the day or week, even when they aren't actually experiencing anything similar at all! This means that people living with Complex PTSD often find themselves unable to move on.

SYMPTOMS OF COMPLEX PTSD

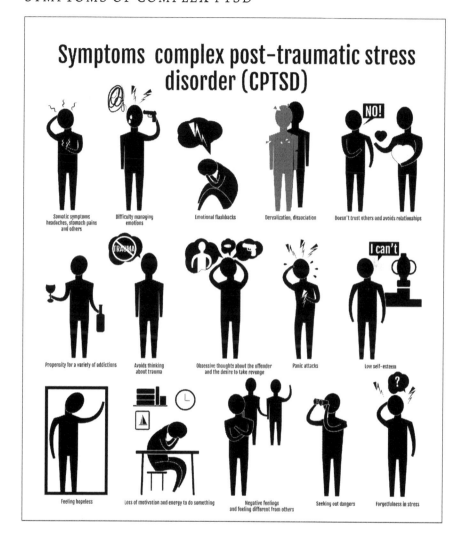

Complex PTSD manifests in several ways depending on the specific individual characteristics such as age, sex, type of trauma e.t.c. In addition to this, the symptoms these individuals present may also include symptoms commonly attributed to PTSD such as flashbacks, nightmares, anxiety attacks, etc. As a result, complex PTSD can be difficult to diagnose or often confused with PTSD.

The symptoms of this condition may vary among people of different age groups, such as children, teenagers, and adults. Due to this, we will be discussing these symptoms differently amongst different age groups.

Complex PTSD Symptoms in Children and Teenagers

Some of the symptoms of Complex PTSD seen in children and adolescents include:

Poor and Dysregulated Physical Development

Children who have been exposed to prolonged debilitating and traumatic events may have difficulties interpreting stimuli from their sense organs. This may further result in sensory-motor developmental deficits that may manifest as an overreaction or underreaction to encountered stimuli. Hence, these children may have challenges achieving milestones and performing physical activities such as speaking, maintaining a good posture, and writing which are expected for their ages.

Even if the child has achieved this milestone, it may be discovered that after such traumatic events occur, the child may regress and lose these milestones. It has also been discovered that these children are prone to developing medical conditions when compared to their counterparts. This may be attributed to the dysregulation of hormone production in Complex PTSD that culminates in the abnormal physical and immunologic development of the child.

Dysfunctional Emotional Development and Adaptation

Children who have been in constant exposure to traumatic events typically have trouble identifying and conveying emotions as well as expressing their needs and wants. They may also have challenges discerning and acknowledging others' emotional needs and states. For instance, a 10-year-old child who is expected to know how to say no in situations they do not find appealing may find this difficult to do. On the other hand, he or she may also get uncontrollably agitated and lash out in anger.

This dysregulation in emotional control and development may end up causing the child to develop problems with creating and respecting boundaries, a lack of trust in humans, social seclusion, challenges with behavioral control that can lead to a lack of impulse control, aggression, pathological self-soothing, unhealthy coping mechanisms, and sleep difficulties.

Poor Self-Esteem and Self-Concept Development

Children and adolescents who are victims of chronic exposure to traumatic events often develop low self-esteem, guilt, and shame and view themselves in a negative light. Some may even end up believing that they deserved to suffer the horrible experiences they have been put through.

Poor Neurological and Cognitive Development

A good number of children with complex PTSD may end up developing neurological and cognitive deficits that make it difficult to learn and participate in various logical and analytical functions. Some of these deficits include attention deficit disorders, dissociative personality disorders, etc. As a result, they may struggle to perform tasks that require focus, planning, and basic thinking.

Complex PTSD Symptoms in Adults

Adults may develop Complex PTSD stemming from exposure to prolonged trauma in childhood or experiences in adulthood. Adults with Complex PTSD may exhibit the following symptoms:

Changes in Consciousness

Individuals with Complex PTSD often exhibit an altered state of consciousness or dissociative behaviors. This may arise directly from the trauma or as a means to cope with the overwhelming emotions and memories of the event. These feelings may manifest as a lack of concentration and focus, difficulty in remembering key details of the events, intrusive memories and flashbacks of the event, and episodes where they feel like observers or detached from their everyday lives.

Defective Expression and Regulation of Emotions

Because of the overwhelming nature of the feelings and emotions people with Complex PTSD deal with, these individuals may find it difficult to make sense of these emotions and control them. These may manifest as sudden mood swings, abrupt outbursts of anger, and persistent feelings of sadness and depression.

Changes in Self-Esteem and Self-Perception

It is common for individuals who have experienced terrible incidents for a long time to develop negative perceptions about themselves. This is particularly prevalent in people who have experienced one form of abuse or the other. These individuals develop intense feelings of guilt, shame, defilement, stigma, and being completely different or isolated from other human beings.

Changes in Relationships with Others

Individuals dealing with Complex PTSD find it difficult to relate, trust and form connections with other people. Due to the hyper-arousal and hypervigilance symptoms such as persistent fear and feeling of danger, these individuals automatically believe that everyone is out to hurt them. Hence, this hinders them from building new, meaningful relationships or even maintaining the ones they have with their loved ones.

Unhealthy Perceptions and Preoccupation with the Abuser.

This is also commonly seen in individuals who went through one form of abuse or the other. These individuals tend to develop a fixation and obsess over their abusers. This obsession may either take the form of revenge or unhealthy affection and devotion for the abuser.

Changes in Systems of Meaning

Following prolonged exposure to a traumatic event, there is often a change in how the individual views the world as a whole. For example, victims who were known to be strongly religious may completely lose faith in their religions. These individuals become apathetic to their surroundings and develop a strong sense of despair or hopelessness about the world.

Other physical symptoms include:

- Difficulty in breathing or fast breathing
- Poor or increased appetite
- Excessive sweating
- Changes in sleep patterns
- Dizziness
- Unexplained pains and aches.

CAUSES OF COMPLEX PTSD

There are no specific causes of Complex PTSD because while some individuals may experience certain traumatic events and develop the condition, others may not. Hence, the development of Complex PTSD is dependent on the individual and the stage in life in which the incident was experienced. However, Complex PTSD is believed to stem from prolonged and repeated exposure to some of these events:

Abuse

This is perhaps the most common cause of Complex PTSD in both adults and children. Abuse is an act that is purposely aimed at harming an individual. It spans different scopes including:

- Physical abuse
- Verbal abuse
- Sexual assault and Rape

- Emotional abuse
- Psychological abuse
- Elder abuse
- Domestic abuse and violence
- Financial abuse
- Spiritual abuse.

In the United States, it is estimated that approximately one in three women and one in five men have been reported to have suffered from one form of abuse from a familiar individual in their lifetime. Hence, this goes to say that abuse is often perpetuated by someone close to the victim. The aim of abuse is to exercise control over another individual hence, it is one of the greatest crimes against humanity. The negative effects of abuse on both children and adults can not be ignored as

Neglect or Abandonment

This is commonly seen during childhood when children are abandoned or fail to receive the all-around care, attention, and support they require to develop optimally. This may result in unfavorable outcomes stretching from defective physical and cognitive development in childhood to developing dangerous coping mechanisms, harmful behaviors, and poor social and emotional behaviors later on in life.

War Experiences

This encompasses individuals living in war-stricken regions, prisoners of war, or people who have fought in wars. Experiences such as this tend to alter the core human psyche, leading to the development of Complex PTSD because there is an increase in the occurrence of violent acts during war. In addition to the inevitable loss of life and horrors associated with fighting in a war that is experienced by the soldiers, the next targets of war are civilians, particularly women and children.

Inhumane acts such as rape, the use of humans as shields, mass genocides, torture, lack of access to basic amenities e.t.c are the order of the day. Children who are found in such regions are often killed and those who survive are often orphaned and abandoned, leaving them exposed to horrors such as being used as sex workers, brutalized, or having to engage in dangerous acts to carve out a living.

Soldiers, prisoners of war, and refugees often find it difficult to blend into society due to the horrors they have witnessed. Many of them have nightmares and flashbacks of the war events, develop persistent fear and anxiety disorders, or even unnatural coping mechanisms such as aggression, dissociative amnesia e.t.c just to cope with the aftermath of war.

Slavery and Human Trafficking

Survivors of slavery and human trafficking typically experience overwhelming psychological aftermaths during and after their experience. These experiences are usually associated with activities that are aimed at debasing and stripping humans of their base humanity and rights. These horrendous acts which these individuals are subjected to cause them to develop anxiety, depression, extreme fear and guilt and other symptoms of mental trauma.

These individuals may even turn to addictive substances like illicit drugs and self-destructive habits to find succor from the overwhelming feelings they usually experience, even after several years following the original event.

Risk Factors for Developing Complex PTSD

In addition to experiencing these debilitating events, certain risk factors predispose an individual to develop Complex PTSD. They include:

- The onset of trauma in childhood
- A history of alcohol and substance abuse

- A history of an underlying mental illness
- Lack of adequate support following the event
- Stigmatization especially in cases of abuse
- Developing a poor coping mechanism to deal with the outcome of the event
- Stress from other aspects of the individual's life.

TRIGGERS OF COMPLEX PTSD

Symptoms and behavioral episodes associated with Complex PTSD can be stimulated by a variety of catalysts. These triggers include:

- Sounds, voices, and songs that remind them of the traumatic events they experienced
- Smells that remind them of the traumatic events they experienced
- Images from the past or present that remind them of the traumatic events they experienced
- Locations that are similar to or remind them of the traumatic events they experienced
- Conversations that remind them of the traumatic events they experienced
- People that remind them of the traumatic events they experienced

Once an individual with Complex PTSD is exposed to any trigger closely associated with the traumatic event, it initiates a chain of occurrences similar to the original event. The amygdala, which is overly sensitive at this point, is unable to fully discern that the individual is not in danger and instead, interprets the trigger as the traumatic events occurring again. This further results in the symptoms and associated behaviors seen in Complex post-traumatic stress disorders such as nightmares, anxiety attacks, feats of aggression and irrational behaviors etc.

COPING BEHAVIORS OF PEOPLE WITH COMPLEX PTSD

When an individual develops Complex PTSD, it is also likely that he or she would search for ways to cope with the aftermath and symptoms that are associated with Complex PTSD. Because these coping mechanisms are unique and tailored to the individual and the experience, they may either be positive or negative. Another thing to note is that while a coping mechanism may be considered negative to one person, it may also be considered positive to another person.

Positive Coping Mechanisms of People with Complex PTSD

While it may not be easy to adopt healthy and positive behaviors, doing so is one of the first steps to properly managing the aftermath and symptoms of Complex PTSD. Here are some positive coping mechanisms to ameliorate the effects of Complex PTSD:

Exercising

The benefits of exercise especially for an individual suffering from Complex PTSD can not be overlooked. Exercise provides an excellent avenue to deal with the effects of prolonged trauma as it decreases stress levels and feelings of anxiety while it increases feelings of relaxation by stimulating the body to release endorphins and generally improves your mood and sleep pattern that is often disrupted by the effects of trauma.

As little as a 20-minute walk in nature daily does wonders for individuals trying to cope with complex PTSD. Other forms of exercise that can help in coping with Complex PTSD include yoga, running, swimming, biking, and playing games like basketball, tennis e.t.c. It is important to note that while exercise is a good coping mechanism, it should be done in moderation. Do not overstretch your body's limits and always take care of yourself when you exercise to avoid compounding the already present issues.

Breathing and Relaxation Exercises

Deep and focused breathing is another great method to relax and cope with Complex PTSD. Deep breathing and relaxation help to decrease stress levels and feelings of anxiety by stimulating the brain which in turn increases oxygen supply and perfusion, reduces blood pressure, slows heart rate, and releases any tension in your body.

These physical changes ultimately improve the individual's mental state and help to bring him or her into a state of mindfulness.

Talking

Talking about a difficult or traumatic experience with a loved one, a therapist, or within a support group has been known to help individuals with Complex PTSD. Confiding in a trusted individual, individuals with similar experiences, or a professional therapist, expressing how you feel about the situation helps to manage stress and anxiety by releasing suppressed feelings.

It allows you to feel these emotions without getting overwhelmed, instead of stifling them as this is known to manifest in even more destructive ways. Positive affirmations can also serve as tools for coping with Complex PTSD. Speaking positive words into your life and reminding yourself that you are not a product of the trauma you faced helps to boost your mood, lessen negative thoughts, and decrease anxiety and stress. It also improves your self-esteem and body image and helps you develop a more optimistic outlook toward life.

Eating Healthy, Nutritious Foods

There is a saying that you are what you eat hence, maintaining a healthy diet gives your body the nutrients it needs to heal both the physical and mental traumas the body might have suffered. Recently, it has been discovered that eating healthy nutritious food has a positive effect on the mechanisms involved in developing Complex PTSD. Hence, it helps to improve mood and reduce feelings of anxiety and stress while promoting feelings of happiness.

In addition, individuals with mental disorders such as Complex PTSD have a higher risk of developing chronic illnesses such as cardiovascular disease, diabetes e.t.c. Thus, nutrient-rich food provides the necessary nutrients required to heal the body and boost the immune system.

Prioritizing Adequate Rest and Sleep

Adequate rest and sleep give the brain and the body the ability to properly process the feelings they may be experiencing. This creates an avenue for healing and also improves mental health, increases focus, concentration and memory, and improves the individual's immune system.

Finding a New Hobby

Developing a new hobby like dancing, singing, reading, cooking, knitting, drawing and painting greatly helps to manage the stressful emotions and feelings that come with Complex PTSD. Engaging in activities you enjoy releases endorphins and feelings of happiness that improve your mood and reduce feelings of stress and anxiety.

Finding a new hobby also keeps you occupied and reduces the time you might spend ruminating over the incident. It also gives you a sense of accomplishment and helps you discover more about yourself and your strength thus, helping you develop a positive perception of yourself.

Negative Coping Mechanisms of People with Complex PTSD

A good number of individuals with Complex PTSD often try to deal with the problems they are facing by developing certain maladaptive behaviors. While some of these behaviors might offer a temporary solution and relief at the beginning,

Alcohol and Substance Use

Many individuals with Complex PTSD turn to alcohol and substance use to deal with the effects of prolonged trauma. This is because alcohol and substances like tobacco, and narcotics provide a temporary reprieve from the reality that a person with Complex PTSD has to deal with. These substances increase feelings of pleasure, and relaxation, decrease feelings of stress and anxiety and remove one's inhibitions, instead of dealing with the root of the problem.

Because of these qualities, heavy drinking and misuse of prescription or illegal drugs become an avenue that the individual turns towards to get away from the overwhelming challenges the individual might be facing.

Self Harm

While most people may consider self-harm or non-suicidal self-injury as a mental disorder, it is most times a negative coping mechanism people develop to deal with the aftermaths of repeated trauma. Self-harm is when an individual inflicts pain and injuries by cutting, burning, scratching, flogging, pulling out their hair or hitting themselves in a way to cope with the overpowering effects of the trauma they faced.

The physical pain felt creates a distraction or masks the larger and deeper negative feelings associated with Complex PTSD. Furthermore, pain also causes the body to release endorphins that are responsible for mood change. With this, the individual has temporary relief from these negative feelings and mental stress suffered by the individual.

Aggressive Reactions

Individuals dealing with Complex PTSD often develop aggressive and hostile tendencies as coping mechanisms to deal with the aftermath of repeated trauma. He or she tends to be hypervigilant and ends up lashing out at the slightest uncomfortable situation they find themselves in because the brain misinterprets such situations as threats and possible repetitions of the trauma.

These aggressive tendencies may also stem from the negative self-perception the individual has about him or herself.

Poor Food Habits

Individuals with Complex PTSD may develop poor feeding habits- either binge eating or a lack of eating- as a means to cope with the negative effects of the condition. Such individuals may resort to food and excess eating for comfort and temporary relief from the painful experience.

It is also important to remember that trauma causes individuals to have a negative self-perception and experience a strong sense of guilt and shame. This can further manifest as body dysmorphia which would cause them to eat less.

Avoidant Behaviors

Individuals who suffer from Complex PTSD often develop conscious or unconscious efforts to avoid dealing with stressful thoughts and situations. This is also often accompanied by people-pleasing behaviors, evading confrontations, refusal to pick up calls or entertain visits, etc.

Ignoring or avoiding problems and stressful situations may provide a short-term solace, however, in the long run, this may not only compound the stressful feelings but may ultimately result in the individual developing more dangerous habits to cope.

Impulsive Behaviors

It is common among people who have experienced chronic trauma to experience a change in behavior and overall temperament that is usually associated with them. This is due to the dysregulation of emotions commonly seen in Complex PTSD. For instance, a person who is naturally very careful and thorough could end up spending a huge amount of money at a go on something frivolous like gambling.

Such individuals may also begin driving recklessly, picking up unnecessary fights with random people, etc. All these uncontrolled behaviors are the individual's attempt at filling up the void created within them and coping with the overwhelming feelings that come with Complex PTSD.

PTSD

While both conditions are closely related, Post Traumatic Stress Disorder and Complex Post Traumatic Stress Disorder describe different psychological disorders that have different ways of development, modes of treatment, effects on individuals, etc.

When an individual experiences a harmful or stressful event, the amygdala of the limbic system in the brain is stimulated and this in turn activates the sympathetic and parasympathetic systems to work hand in hand to help the body adapt and provide the necessary response to the situation.

However, in PTSD, the harmony between these systems is overridden, leading to the formulation of deep neurological patterns and impressions in the brain that can last for long periods after the original event. The amygdala remains hyperactive while the hippocampal control of the amygdala is repressed. This leads to the misinterpretation of stimuli and continuous misperception that the event is happening again, placing the body in a constant "fight, freeze or flight" state.

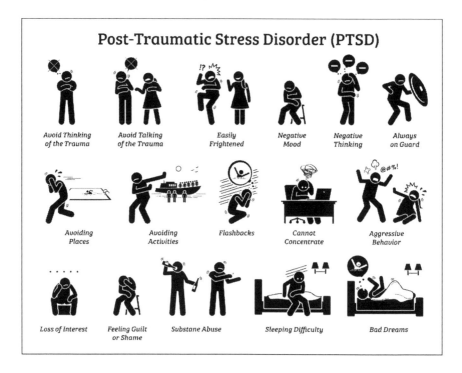

It has also been discovered that people with PTSD have diminished brain activity in areas of the brain that are linked to the understanding and regulation of emotion. These areas include the dorsal and rostral anterior cingulate cortices and the ventromedial prefrontal cortex.

WHAT IS PTSD?

Post Traumatic Stress Disorder (PTSD), also known as traumatic stress reaction, is a psychological and mental disorder that stems from experiencing or witnessing a single traumatic event.

The development of PTSD is dependent on several factors such as age, duration, and severity of trauma because not everyone who experiences a devastating event develops this condition. Studies have shown that in the United States, approximately 3.5% of adults have PTSD yearly and 9% of people develop it at some point in their life. It is also believed to occur more frequently in women than it does in men.

PTSD is a serious condition that can affect anyone at any time -even those who have never been in any life-threatening situation or people who aren't the victims themselves. People who develop PTSD without being the victims are more likely to have experienced a situation that involved:

- Being exposed to someone else's traumatic event, such as watching a violent crime
- Being responsible for someone else's traumatic event
- Being in charge of caring for a victim of trauma, such as serving as a first responder during an emergency situation

PTSD is characterized by one or more psychological reactions to the event, such as anxiety, avoidance, nightmares, flashbacks, irritability, depression, anxiety, difficulty sleeping or concentrating on daily tasks that persist for months or years after the event. These symptoms are often accompanied by physical reactions like increased heart rate, muscle tension and sweating.

PTSD causes the sufferer to feel an overwhelming sense of fear, helplessness, horror or depression after the event. People who develop PTSD may have trouble functioning in their daily lives. They may struggle to maintain relationships and deal with ordinary stressors like school, work and finances. They may develop depression and substance use disorders in addition to PTSD. In some cases, people with PTSD become suicidal.

Anybody who goes through a trauma is at risk of developing PTSD. Some people are more vulnerable than others. If you've experienced trauma in the past, you're at greater risk of experiencing it again in the future and reacting strongly to it. Also, if someone has been exposed to significant stressors on a regular basis over many years, such as war, they're also at greater risk of developing PTSD than those who haven't been exposed this way.

Relationships with loved ones can also affect your risk of developing PTSD; people with strong support systems, such as parents who take an active role in monitoring their children's behavior and helping them make positive decisions are less likely to develop the disorder after going through trauma than those without such networks.

HOW DOES COMPLEX PTSD DIFFER FROM PTSD

The major difference between PTSD and complex PTSD is the duration and frequency of exposure to traumatic events. Post-traumatic stress disorder develops from experiencing or witnessing a single traumatic event such as a ghastly accident or the death of a loved one. On the other hand, Complex post-traumatic stress disorder requires repeated and prolonged exposure to an extremely traumatic events such as abuse, war, slavery and human trafficking.

In addition, the manifestations and symptoms of Complex PTSD are more complicated than that of PTSD, hence, the treatment of Complex PTSD is more intricate and requires a longer period with more frequent appointments. It also requires creating opportunities for these persons to build various skills to enable them to fully integrate into society. Furthermore, unlike PTSD where medications such as antidepressants like sertraline and anti-anxiety medications like clonazepam may be used, there is currently no medication precisely recommended for Complex PTSD.

CAUSES OF POST-TRAUMATIC STRESS DISORDER

As previously reiterated, PTSD occurs from a singular experience or witness of a distressing event. Here are some of the events that may cause an individual to develop PTSD:

- Terrible, ghastly accidents

- Loss of a loved one
- Traumatic birth experiences
- Sexual assault
- Severe abuse of any form
- Natural disasters.

Individuals with any of the following are more likely to develop PTSD after encountering a traumatic event:

- A history of mental illness
- Lack of adequate care and support following the traumatic experience
- A history of drug or substance use.

SYMPTOMS OF POST TRAUMATIC STRESS DISORDER

PTSD and Complex PTSD share similarities in their mode of manifestation since both conditions arise due to an encounter with a distressing event that culminates in alterations in the neurohormonal interpretation and regulation of stimulation.

Some of these symptoms include:

- Distressing flashbacks and nightmares about what happened during the traumatic incident
- Hyper-arousal, which occurs when you're constantly on edge, feeling activated and ready to run at any second despite being in a safe environment
- Sleep disturbance such as insomnia or somnolence
- A feeling of detachment from others due to an inability to connect with them on an emotional level
- Lack of focus and concentration
- Intense aggressive and hostile behaviors
- Difficult behavior in children and adolescents

- Persistent and overwhelming feelings of fear, guilt, shame, anxiety, and isolation
- Avoidant behaviors such as people-pleasing, avoiding distressing situations, etc.
- Physical symptoms, such as headaches, dizziness, chest pains and stomach aches
- Self-destructive behaviors such as alcohol and substance abuse, self-harming
- Impulsive and risky behaviors
- Emotional numbness or inability to feel emotions especially positive emotions, such as joy, hope, or enthusiasm
- Apathy or loss of interest in activities one previously enjoyed.
- Anxiety and/or depression
- Feeling nervous or on edge
- Being easily startled or startled easily
- Having trouble with concentration and memory
- Feeling aggressive or irritable -people with ptsd may become easily irritated and angry at small things that usually wouldn't bother them before they had trauma

MANAGEMENT OF POST TRAUMATIC STRESS DISORDER

The management of PTSD is a combination therapy of psychotherapy and pharmacotherapy.

Psychotherapy

One of the strongest and most effective strategies in the management of PTSD is counseling. It encompasses both behavioral and cognitive-behavioral remedies such as:

Prolonged Exposure Therapy

This is a form of behavioral and cognitive therapy that helps individuals to gradually approach trauma-related memories, feelings and situations by consciously rehashing the event and then facing these conditions, places, and things that remind them of the trauma or make them feel unsafe.

Cognitive Processing Therapy

This, on the other hand, is a distinct type of cognitive behavioral therapy that helps individuals learn how to deal with and change undesirable beliefs associated with the trauma. Naturally, the feelings and emotions accompanying PTSD are generally very negative and difficult to cope with hence, the individual may develop avoidant coping mechanisms that can hinder the natural process of dealing with the traumatic event and their recovery.

Thus, cognitive processing therapy helps them to accurately process the memory of the traumatic event and the emotions stemming from this event, in turn, facilitating their healing process.

Eye Movement Desensitization and Reprocessing (EMDR)

This form of psychotherapy utilizes bilateral stimulation to help the individual work through the traumatic experience. This form of therapy uses bilateral stimulation, typically eye movements while urging the individual to focus on the memory of the trauma. This in turn helps the individual to process the traumatic events by reducing how strongly they remember and feel emotions associated with the trauma memories.

Other approaches include family therapy, support groups and group therapy e.t.c.

Medication

Some of the medications used in the management of PTSD include:

- Antidepressants such as amitriptyline and isocarboxazid
- Selective serotonin reuptake inhibitors (SSRIs) such as citalopram, fluoxetine, paroxetine and sertraline.

Certain medications can be used to control particular symptoms like:

- Nightmares: Prazosin may be used to decrease the occurrence of distressing nightmares
- Sleep disturbances: Clonidine may be prescribed
- Propranolol is administered to help lessen the development of traumatic memories.

3

TRAUMA

*I*n this chapter, we'll be discussing the root of the entire problem: trauma.

When you think about it, trauma is the crux of the entire complex PTSD, because without trauma, there will be no condition such as PTSD or complex PTSD. Trauma is a complex topic, but our goal is to keep it simple. It's common for people who have experienced traumatic events, such as sexual assault or military combat to develop feelings of distress in response. Trauma can affect your ability to trust friends and family members, as well as yourself and your own perception of reality.

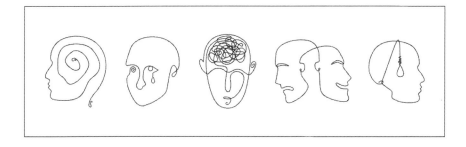

As human beings, we live in a world full of stress. We are constantly exposed to a multitude of stimuli that can be both positive and negative. One such stimulus is the trauma or abuse that some people experience throughout their lifetime. Trauma is an emotional response that occurs when you are exposed to something threatening or dangerous. The body's reaction to this event is called post traumatic stress disorder or complex post-traumatic stress disorder that has been discussed above.

WHAT IS TRAUMA?

When you think of trauma, what comes to mind? The images of war, grief, and fear that we see in our newsfeeds. The stories we hear about the horrors people have experienced. But what about the trauma that doesn't make headlines? What about the stressors that happen every day -the ones that don't capture national attention but still have a huge impact on your life? How do they play out in the lives of veterans and their families?

Trauma is a psychological response to an event that can cause intense emotional pain. Traumatic events are those that cause severe psychological distress and can be caused by many different things. Trauma causes changes in the brain that last for months or years after the initial event occurred. The consequence of this is that even months later, when the individual does not remember what happened, the body remembers it! The body remembers the exact sensations it felt during the traumatic event and uses those memories to prepare for further danger when it perceives a similar situation arising again.

Although trauma can occur at any age, it has particularly debilitating long-term effects on children's developing brains. Although in children, trauma may fade away as they grow older, the lasting effects usually follow them into adulthood.

ACUTE STRESS DISORDER

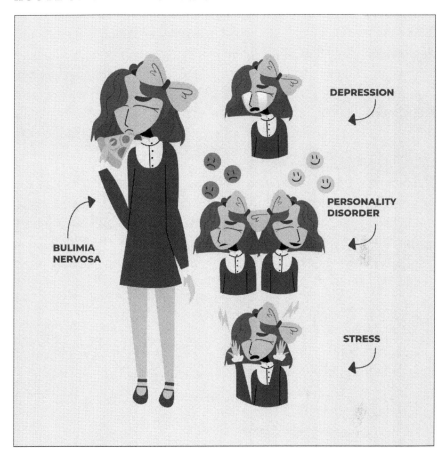

It is important to know that everyone reacts to trauma differently. While many people who experience trauma will recover and not develop PTSD, others will find it more difficult to recover, and may develop PTSD or complex PTSD. Some people will develop certain symptoms of trauma that may fade away in weeks. When this happens, it is known as acute stress disorder.

Acute stress disorder (ASD) is an anxiety disorder that occurs after a person experiences a traumatic event. It's characterized by the sudden onset of intense fear or anxiety and can lead to physical symptoms like sweating, rapid heartbeat, muscle twitching, nausea, and trouble sleeping.

There are two types of ASD: acute stress disorder due to trauma and adjustment disorder. Both share the symptom of intense fear or anxiety in response to a specific stressful event or series of events. But there is a difference in how long the symptoms last -people with adjustment disorder may experience them for months, while people with acute stress disorder due to trauma might have them for only one day.

It's important to note that acute stress disorder (ASD) is not the same thing as post-traumatic stress disorder (PTSD). In fact, there are many people who have experienced both ASD and PTSD. Those with ASD tend to feel intense distress after an event that triggered it, but they don't have flashbacks or nightmares as part of their syndrome.

Some of the symptoms are:

- Intense fear
- Difficulty sleeping
- Increased heart rate or breathing
- Irritability
- Feeling out of control overwhelmed
- Being unable to focus on anything but the situation or event that caused the disorder
- Feeling anxious, irritable, or even panicky

People with ASD are often able to work through their symptoms without seeking professional help from mental health professionals such as psychologists or psychiatrists.

CAUSES OF TRAUMA

Trauma is a complicated condition. It can be caused by a number of different events and it's not always easy to figure out what caused it. Here are some of the most common causes of trauma:

Physical trauma

Traumatic incidents that result in physical harm, such as being hit by a car or stabbed with a knife, are sometimes called "accidents." However, there are many factors that can make these events more than just accidents: for example, if someone is injured in an accident and then develops PTSD or depression as a result of their experience, this may be considered an accident even though it was not intended.

Emotional trauma

Emotional trauma includes any incident that causes severe emotional distress or fear for yourself or others. This might include sexual abuse (either physically or emotionally), domestic violence, bullying at school, or other similar incidents that might be upsetting to you or someone close to you.

SYMPTOMS OF TRAUMA

Trauma is a common occurrence in life. It can occur due to many reasons, and can have a wide range of effects on the person experiencing it.

In order to understand trauma, it is important to first understand how our bodies work. Our bodies are made up of organs that perform different functions at different times. For example, when someone sneezes, their body releases air into the lungs and throat, which then forces them to cough out any foreign objects that got caught in their nose or throat. This is called an involuntary response because we do not choose when these things happen—they just happen without us having control over them.

Our brains also work similarly; they are constantly processing information from our senses (sight, sound, touch) and from other parts of our bodies (muscles). When we experience something traumatic or stressful, this process can be interrupted by an electrochemical reaction called "fear" which causes us to freeze in place or flee from whatever caused us fear. This can lead to physiological changes such as increased heart rate and blood pressure as well as changes in breathing patterns which may cause shortness of breath or even hyperventilation if severe enough.

If you or someone you know has experienced trauma, it's important to remember that no two people respond to trauma in the same way. While some may have a more open and obvious response to traumatic events, some may crawl into their shells, while others may go about their days like nothing happened. This may make it difficult for you to determine if someone has trauma or not.

Physical Symptoms

- Dizziness
- Nausea
- Change in sleep patterns
- Headaches and body aches
- Gastrointestinal complications
- Change in appetite
- Sleep problems

Emotional Symptoms

In addition to these physical symptoms, people may also experience the following emotional symptoms:

- Anger toward themselves (self-blame)

- Embarrassment/humiliation over what happened during the trauma event
- Guilt over not being able to stop what happened from happening
- Denial
- Sadness or moodiness
- Feelings of numbness or detachment from one's surroundings
- A sense of helplessness and powerlessness
- Fearfulness about the future
- Increased irritability with others around them
- Inability to trust friends, family members, oneself and others
- Doubts about one's perception of reality
- Feelings of hopelessness and depression,

Psychological Symptoms

- Depression
- Anxiety
- PTSD
- ASD
- Complex PTSD
- Substance abuse problems

TRAUMA AND THE LINK TO MENTAL HEALTH

Trauma is a word that strikes fear into the hearts of many people. It's often used as the justification for why someone can't control their emotions or behavior, but most times, trauma is not the cause of mental health conditions. Instead, it just compounds the effects of past and ongoing exposure to stressors on a person's brain development.

Trauma can be a symptom of mental health conditions, or it can cause a mental health condition. In other words, trauma can contribute to the development of a mental health condition and may even be the cause.

For example: A person has been sexually abused as a child and develops PTSD (post-traumatic stress disorder). They are also diagnosed with bipolar disorder because they have mood swings caused by their trauma.

Another way trauma can affect mental health is through hormone imbalance. Negative life events lead to changes in a person's hormone balance, immune system, and stress response. Exposure to stress hormones can disrupt brain development and lead to long-term changes in a person's hormone balance. This can lead to problems with memory, sleep, mood and behavior. Trauma survivors are at higher risk for depression because of the impact that trauma has on their immune system and stress response. They also have trouble feeling empathy, trust and compassion for others as well as themselves.

Stress hormones can disrupt brain development when exposed during childhood or adolescence, including the hippocampus and amygdala. These areas of the brain are involved in memory formation, as well as decision making and impulse control.

When you're stressed out from a traumatic event or experience, your body releases cortisol -a stress hormone- in an attempt to help you cope with the situation. But over time this may cause problems for your mental health because it can disrupt sleep patterns, learning abilities and memory function.

A trauma survivor's brain is wired differently than the brain of a person who has not experienced severe trauma.

- They have a heightened sense of fear, which can make them easily startled and unable to sleep properly.
- Their ability to concentrate and remember details is also impaired because they are so easily distracted by their own

thoughts or feelings that they don't notice things going on around them (or don't care).
- This can lead to memory problems for survivors like lapses in attention span or not being able to recall events from long ago but still having vivid memories from an incident that happened just yesterday.

It's important to note that while trauma is a risk factor for developing certain types of mental illness, it isn't the only risk factor or even necessarily the most significant one. In fact, some people who experience severe trauma may never develop any symptoms at all, so don't assume that someone who has been through something traumatic must have PTSD!

It's also important not to confuse what was done with us versus how we feel about ourselves as individuals because even though our brains may react differently after experiencing trauma, this doesn't mean those flashbacks make us worse than others because they're still our own thoughts and feelings. It just means there's an internal struggle going on inside our heads too!

RECOVERING FROM COMPLEX PTSD: DIAGNOSIS AND TREATMENT

*D*iagnosing and beginning the management of Complex PTSD can be an arduous endeavor, especially for the person involved. It takes courage and the will to improve one's life to take the first step in seeking help. While the journey to healing requires effort and does not happen overnight, there are tips, tools and interventions that can help individuals diagnosed with PTSD and Complex PTSD to live better lives.

But first, we would discuss how the diagnosis of PTSD is made.

HOW IS THE DIAGNOSIS OF POST TRAUMATIC STRESS DISORDER MADE

The diagnosis of Post Traumatic Stress Disorder is multifaceted and can only be made after at least one month following the traumatic event. The diagnosis of PTSD begins with a detailed medical history and physical evaluation carried out by a physician. This is to rule out the possibility of other underlying mental and neurological disorders or the effects of substance use.

According to the International Classification of Diseases and Related Health Problems 10 (ICD-10), PTSD has been described as a "Reaction to severe stress, and adjustment disorders." Thus, because of this and the relative novelty of PTSD and Complex PTSD in the medical field, the Board of Trustees of the American Psychiatric Association (APA) drew up an extensively revised criteria for diagnosing PTSD. This led to the development of the fifth edition of the Diagnostic and Statistical Manual of Mental Disorders (DSM-5) criteria for diagnosing PTSD include:

Criterion A: Stressor (traumatic event)

The individual has to have been exposed to an extremely traumatic event such as death, threatened death or injury, actual or threatened serious injury, actual sexual violence, threatened sexual violence, loss of a loved e.t.c in any of the following ways:

- Direct encounter or experience
- Witnessing the trauma
- Discovering that a loved one experienced such an event
- Indirect exposure to unpleasant details of the trauma, typically during professional duties such as medical professionals, first responders, firefighters e.t.c

Criterion B: Intrusive Symptoms

The traumatic event is consistently re-experienced in the following ways and for a diagnosis of PTSD to be made, at least one is required:

- Undesirable and disconcerting memories
- Flashbacks
- Nightmares
- Emotional distress following an encounter with traumatic triggers

- Increased physical reactivity following an encounter with traumatic triggers.

Criterion C: Avoidance

Following the traumatic event, the individual tries to avoid trauma-related triggers in the following ways and at least one is required to make a diagnosis:

- Trauma-related thoughts or feelings such as wishful thinking, maladaptive daydreaming, burying emotions,
- Trauma-related external reminders by Canceling plans last minute, not answering calls or texts, and avoiding certain people and places at certain times.

Criterion D: Negative Alterations in Cognitions and Mood

Individuals who have experienced extreme and traumatic events typically develop negative thoughts or feelings which manifest in the following ways. At least two are required to make a diagnosis:

- Difficulty or inability to recall important details of the trauma
- Extremely negative thoughts and perceptions pertaining to oneself or the world
- Persistent feelings of guilt, shame and blame of oneself or others for causing the trauma
- Negative affect
- Apathy or decreased interest in activities one previously enjoyed
- Persistent feelings of isolation
- Difficulty in experiencing or expressing positive affect or emotions.

Criterion E: Alterations in Arousal and Reactivity

Individuals who have experienced extreme and traumatic events typically experience trauma-related hyperarousal and reactivity that typically manifest in the following ways:

- Irritability or aggressive behaviors
- Destructive or unpredictable behavior
- Difficulty in or a lack of concentration and focus
- Hypervigilance
- Sleep disturbances
- Exacerbated startle response.

Criterion F: Duration

Before a diagnosis of PTSD can be made, the symptoms must have lasted for at least four weeks following the traumatic event.

Criterion G: Functional significance

Before PTSD can be diagnosed in an individual, it is required and must have been observed that the presence of these symptoms has adversely affected the individual's quality of life. The individual may be unable to properly carry out his or her regular activities i.e social activities of occupational duties e.t.c.

Criterion H: Exclusion

Before a diagnosis of PTSD can be made in an individual, a thorough assessment must be carried out to ensure that the symptoms present are not due to medication, substance misuse or other underlying illnesses.

In addition to the above criteria, the individual must experience increased levels of any of the following in reaction to trauma-related stimuli:

Dissociative Specification

This includes:

- Depersonalization: Feelings of detachment from oneself or occurrences whereby the individual feels he or she is an external observer of his or her life and surroundings
- Derealization. Experience of unreality, distance, or distortion such as doubting the authenticity of an experience happening to the person.

Delayed Specification

For a full diagnosis of PTSD to be made, assessment and observation should be carried out for at least six months following the trauma, even if symptoms begin immediately.

In summary, to make a diagnosis of PTSD, the individual must have at least:

- one re-experiencing symptom
- three avoidance symptoms
- two negative alterations in mood and cognition, and
- two hyperarousal symptoms all for a minimum of four weeks.

The assessment and screening for PTSD encompass a multi-technique examination procedure that involves the use of several physician-administered interviews and instruments to make an official diagnosis of PTSD. Some of these assessment instruments that have proven reliable and valid for PTSD diagnosis according to the DSM-5 diagnosis of PTSD include:

The Clinician-Administered PTSD Scale for the DSM-5 (CAPS-5)

This 30-item questionnaire is the gold standard for diagnosing PTSD. It helps clinicians to make a diagnosis of PTSD by asking questions suitable for evaluating the dissociative aspects of PTSD which include depersonalization and derealization. The questions focus on the:

- onset and duration of symptoms
- subjective distress
- impact of symptoms on individual social and occupational activities
- improvement in symptoms since the last assessment
- comprehensive response validity
- comprehensive PTSD severity.

It has 3 versions that are currently being used in clinical practice and they correspond to different periods. Thus, it can be used to assess:

- Symptoms over the past week
- Symptoms over the past month to make a current diagnosis of PTSD and
- Symptoms of the worst month and make a lifetime diagnosis of PTSD.

Scoring

Each question assesses a symptom using a 5-point scale, with 4 and 5 representing extreme symptoms while 1-2 represents mild symptoms. The CAPS-5 evaluates the severity of the symptoms in the individual by adding up the total scores from each criterion and the higher the score, the more severe the PTSD symptoms are.

Severity Rating Scale of CAPS-5

In addition, CAPS-5 further helps to classify the severity of PTSD into:

- Absent: The individual denies the problem or his or her recount does not fit the DSM-5 symptom criteria for diagnosis
- Mild or subthreshold: The individual illustrates symptoms that conform to the symptom criterion but these symptoms are not severe enough to be deemed clinically significant.

Hence, the problem does not fully meet the DSM-5 symptom criteria and a diagnosis of PTSD can not be made
- Moderate or threshold: The individual describes clinically significant symptoms which fully meet the DSM-5 symptom criterion. In this case, a diagnosis of PTSD can be made and medical intervention is required
- Severe or markedly elevated: In this case, the symptoms described by the individual exceed the standard threshold. They are typically overwhelming and difficult to manage hence, immediate intervention is necessary
- Extreme or incapacitating: The symptoms described and observed in the individual are dramatic, exceeding far above the standard threshold. They are usually pervasive, intractable, and overwhelming, and require high-priority intervention.

The PTSD Symptom Scale Interview (PSS-I-5)

This is another 24-item semi-structured questionnaire that is commonly used to assess and make a diagnosis of PTSD. It evaluates the individual's symptoms of PTSD using the DSM-5 criteria over the past month and groups them based on their severity. To get an estimate of the severity, the administrator adds up the scores obtained during the examination, of which the total score is 51.

The Structured Clinical Interview for DSM-5 - PTSD Module (SCID-5 PTSD Module)

This is a semi-structured instrument used for systematically evaluating and diagnosing PTSD according to the DSM-5 criteria. It has also been employed in other areas such as determining the effectiveness of various treatments for other mental disorders such as depression. Hence, it serves both diagnostic and research purposes. The interview is administered by a doctor or trained mental health specialist who has adequate knowledge about the DSM classification and diagnostic criteria.

The interview subjects may be either individuals with psychiatric disorders, general medical patients or individuals who are not necessarily patients but are participants in a survey of mental illness or relatives of psychiatric patients.

HOW IS COMPLEX POST TRAUMATIC STRESS DISORDER TREATED

PTSD can become chronic if left unaddressed and untreated. The symptoms of PTSD can be mild or severe and may occur within hours to years after exposure to trauma-related events and circumstances. If left untreated, PTSD can lead to depression, anxiety disorders, substance abuse problems and other serious mental health issues.

In order for someone with PTSD to overcome these symptoms they must learn how to manage them through therapy, medication or both. Therapy allows individuals with PTSD sufferers who have experienced trauma-related events/circumstances to understand why they are experiencing these feelings as well as learn coping skills.

We know that when you are dealing with PTSD, it can be difficult to feel like yourself again. It's important to remember that you're not alone -there are lots of resources available to help you get through this process. Asides from support from friends and family members who care about you, you may also need professional help.

The first step in recovering from PTSD is admitting that there is something wrong with your life right now. This may seem like an obvious thing to do but it's important because if you don't admit what's happening then there won't be any change in your life until things get worse and more dangerous situations arise again!

Once you've admitted that there is something wrong with your life now then start talking about it with people who care about you and they will help guide you through this difficult period. Let's take a look at how PTSD can be treated.

SELF-HELP TIPS FOR INDIVIDUALS WITH COMPLEX PTSD

Living with Complex PTSD can be overwhelming sometimes as it can alter a person's emotional, physical, and psychological state in various ways. Hence, even with all the interventions available to manage this condition, it still requires resilience and strength.

However, this does not mean that an individual with Complex PTSD can not live a fulfilling life. But to achieve this, he or she needs to put in the effort and this is why self-care is an important aspect of healing from Complex PTSD. Here are some tips that can help individuals living with Complex PTSD cope and reconnect with life:

Identify Your Triggers

The first step to solving a problem is first recognizing the problem and what caused it. In order to manage the symptoms and aftermath of Complex PTSD, you must first identify the likely things and circumstances that may trigger a relapse. This not only helps you to properly gauge your response and come up with a plan to deal with such situations but it also increases your feeling of control.

Meditation

Individuals living with Complex PTSD typically deal with intrusive and dissociative symptoms as well as feelings of guilt, shame and low self-esteem. Meditation helps the individual to breed feelings of calmness and mindfulness, helping them to be present in the moment as well as create a healthy environment to improve their self-esteem.

Prioritize Getting Adequate Rest and Sleep

Not only is this an excellent coping mechanism but it also helps individuals living with Complex PTSD to improve their quality of life. Adequate rest and sleep give the body ample time to rejuvenate and heal physical and psychological injuries dealt to it.

Engage in Physical Activity

Exercise is a great coping mechanism as well as an excellent way to care for oneself when dealing with Complex PTSD. It helps to boost one's mood and provides a healthy outlet for the negative intrusive feelings that are commonly associated with Complex PTSD while keeping your body in a top, healthy state.

Get a Service Dog

Getting a service dog is another good way to cope with Complex PTSD, especially for individuals who are alone and without family. These animals are trained to identify and satisfy the needs of individuals with Complex PTSD. They assist these individuals and are trained to recognize symptoms such as anxiety and nightmares and to intervene when these symptoms occur, either by seeking help or offering comfort when help is not nearby.

Find a New Hobby

Finding a new activity can help in so many ways when it comes to managing Complex PTSD. Activities like listening to music, singing, drawing, reading e.t.c helps to improve the individual's mood, promote feelings of calmness and provide solace from the overwhelming feelings associated with Complex PTSD.

Maintain a Healthy Diet

As stated earlier, one of the best and most natural ways to ensure the body heals from the effects of prolonged trauma is to ensure that it has enough fuel to do so. Try to increase your consumption of whole foods and grains, fruits, vegetables, nuts, and seeds while limiting your intake of highly processed and sugary foods.

Be Consistent with Treatment

In order to see progress and improvement, it is important for an individual dealing with Complex PTSD to judiciously follow the instructions and advice of their physician. You can not expect to heal the damaging effects of prolonged exposure to trauma in one day. This is why such individuals should keep to their doctor and counseling appointments and utilize all the interventions recommended for the management of this condition.

Confide in a Trusted Individual

Dealing with Complex PTSD may feel isolating and suffocating however, it is important to remember that it is a journey one should not face alone. Always reach out for help, especially when you are struggling to make sense of your feelings and memories. As simple as speaking to a loved one who has consistently shown support goes a long way in helping individuals with Complex PTSD to process and properly deal with these feelings without suppressing them.

HOW YOU CAN AVOID EXACERBATING COMPLEX PTSD AND ITS RELATED COMPLICATIONS

Managing Complex PTSD requires the effort of both the individual and the people close to them in order to achieve the best results possible and give these individuals a chance at a normal life. This is also the aim of management therefore extra care needs to be taken to avoid worsening the already present symptoms and complications. Here are some tips to help you avoid exacerbating the symptoms and complications and complications of Complex PTSD:

Seek Help Immediately

Seeking help and assistance immediately after prolonged exposure to a traumatic event goes a long way in lessening the complications of such exposure and possibly preventing them all together. As little as speaking to a loved one immediately who can then refer you to the appropriate professional help can go a long way in the management as well as in decreasing the complications of Complex PTSD.

Counseling

The role of counseling in the management of Complex PTSD can not be overemphasized as this provides the individual with the environment they require to process the traumatic events and their aftermaths as well as the tools required to give them a shot at a normal life. With counseling, psychological debriefing interventions that are aimed at teaching the individual about normal reactions to trauma and also encouraging them to speak about the event and how they feel can be carried out. Such interventions include:

- Critical incident stress debriefing (CISD)
- Critical incident stress management (CISM)
- Psychological first aid (PFA)
- Cognitive behavior therapy
- Cognitive restructuring therapy
- Exposure based therapy
- Cognitive processing therapy
- Psychoeducation.

Avoid Alcohol and Substance Use

When dealing with Complex PTSD, it is very easy to resort to alcohol, prescription or illegal drugs to numb the overwhelming negative feelings and memories associated with the traumatic event. However, it is crucial to stay away from these as they would not only worsen the already present symptoms by removing your inhibitions and will to continue with your treatment but they can go on to cause other equally damaging problems.

HOW TO AVOID DEVELOPING AVOIDANCE BEHAVIORS TO COPE WITH COMPLEX PTSD

When someone experiences a traumatizing event, it is only natural for them to want to avoid anything that would remind them of the event. Some of the methods resorted to may provide temporary relief from these overwhelming feelings. However, with time these feelings always come back and they may manifest in even more disastrous ways. If you discover that you are developing or using avoidance to deal with a traumatic event, here are some tips to help you reduce this behavior:

Accept your Feelings

It is only natural to have negative feelings after experiencing a devastating event for a long time. Hence, it is important to accept these feelings for what they are and view them as a step towards confronting the traumatic experience and healing. Keeping a journal can go a long way in helping you accept these feelings.

Writing down these negative feelings and sometimes, reading them out loud, helps to explore and confront them. This can give more insight into identifying negative thought patterns, where they stem from and how to manage them.

Recognize what Avoidance Looks Like

The first step to solving a problem is understanding it. Acknowledging what avoidance looks like and why you might be tempted to give in to it would go a long way in helping you avoid developing it as a coping mechanism. In addition, understanding that avoidance may not provide a healthy way to deal with the aftermath of Complex PTSD will encourage you to seek better ways to cope with Complex PTSD.

Practice Exposure

This is all about gradually exposing yourself to each emotion and memory that comes with the event in order to confront them and finally learn to cope with them without breaking down. Select one of these emotions or memories that cause the least amount of anxiety or fear and tolerate it. Attempt to remain in the experience until you begin to feel comfortable and your anxiety reduces. You can use breathing and relaxation techniques to help ground you and ease anxiety.

Seek Professional Help

If you discover you are avoiding dealing with certain emotions, situations or people, especially those that remind you of what you just went through, it is crucial that you seek the help of a therapist. As earlier stated, healing in Complex PTSD does not happen overnight and this makes it more tempting to seek temporary solace and avoid triggers of the event. This is why it is important to enlist the help of someone who can guide you through exploring and confronting these feelings to avoid developing destructive coping mechanisms and ensure you are healing properly.

HOW TO LIVE WITH C-PTSD AND REGAIN EMOTIONAL CONTROL.

Repeatedly experiencing a devastating event can alter an individual psyche and way of life on a core level, putting them at the mercy of the negative emotions and intrusive memories following this event. It can be frightening and can cause such individuals to feel like they are in their own worlds and this further makes it difficult for them to interact with their surroundings. However, as it has been earlier stated, developing Complex PTSD does not automatically mean an individual can not live a happy, meaningful life.

While Complex PTSD can not be cured, with early intervention and the right support from family, support groups as well as professional therapy, it is possible to adequately manage the complications of

Complex PTSD and improve the individual's quality of life. In addition, it is essential to prioritize eating healthy foods, adequate physical exercise, and adequate rest and sleep during the management of Complex PTSD.

Adopting positive coping mechanisms such as meditation, practicing self-soothing activities, positive affirmations, volunteering in your local community e.t.c goes a long way to help you regain your emotional control and live a balanced life. In addition, avoid the use of alcohol and other addictive substances as well as avoidant behaviors that could ultimately hinder your healing process.

BONUS CHAPTER 1

SPECIAL CONTENT: THE POWER OF NOW

The Power of Now

A HANDBOOK ON LETTING GO OF THE PAST AND LIVING IN THE PRESENT

INTRODUCTION

You may be familiar with the phrase "live in the moment." It's a phrase that gets thrown around quite a bit on social media, and it sounds like a great thing to say. But in reality, the phrase is a little deeper than you may think. So what does it mean?

When you live in the present, you're able to observe what's going on around you and make decisions based on what makes sense for your life now -not tomorrow or next week. And while it might sound like an obvious thing to do, many people forget this simple truth when they get caught up in their own lives and forget about how much better things could be if they just took control of themselves instead of letting others take over their lives.

The concept is simple: when you're experiencing something right now and paying attention to it, you can better understand why things happen and make better decisions about your life.

THE POWER OF NOW

A HANDBOOK ON LETTING GO OF THE PAST AND LIVING IN THE PRESENT

LIVING IN THE PRESENT

The present is a great place to be because it's where you can feel the most. When you're in the present moment, there's no need to think about anything except what's happening right now. You don't need to worry about what happened yesterday or tomorrow; you can just enjoy being alive right now and making new memories as they unfold.

You should also be aware of your surroundings -if possible, try not to miss any opportunities for laughter or fun! It's important that we live life fully while we're here on Earth so that when our time comes, we will have had enough of this beautiful planet before leaving it behind forever -which unfortunately happens sooner than most people expect.

It's also important for us as humans to not only survive but thrive during this lifetime too, and one way of doing so would be by living mindfully through all aspects of our lives:

- Physically through activities such as sports participation
- Mentally through activities such as reading books/talks given by experts who share knowledge with others
- Emotionally through activities such as spending time with friends who share similar interests within ourselves, etc.
- Stay in the now!
- Do not dwell on the past. Do not worry about the future.
- Focus only on what you can control, while leaving the rest to fate.
- Stay in the moment and enjoy it!

LETTING GO OF THE PAST

The past is gone, and the future is here yet. That's not a message a lot of people want to hear, but it's true. There are no guarantees about what will happen in your future or how things will turn out for you. But that doesn't mean we can't change our circumstances now! This section is about how letting go of our past can help us solve problems as well as prevent us from getting overwhelmed by life's challenges.

It's important to remember that you can't change the past, but you can change your future. The past is gone and cannot be rewritten - only the future exists now. You might be feeling down about something or someone in your life right now, but if you look at it from a positive POV, many things are good about how things are going for you right now. Maybe this means appreciating what is working well for you; maybe it's time for a new job; maybe it's time to get out of debt; maybe it's time to start saving money again; whatever it is, focus on what works well and use that as motivation instead of dwelling on what doesn't work so well!

You may also find yourself comparing yourself with others who seem happier than you at any given moment. Don't do this! Comparing ourselves with others only leads us down paths where we end up finding ourselves unhappy because we're comparing ourselves against someone else who has more than we do yet still feels worse off than us.

HOW TO LIVE IN THE PRESENT

Life is better when you dwell in the present and make decisions based on what you want to achieve in the future. You're probably familiar with the concept of living in the present, but it can be hard to do when you're being pressured by other people. It helps to remember that there are times when your thoughts should be focused on what you want to achieve in the future.

Here are a few ways to live in the present and make the most of your every moment:

PRACTICE PATIENCE, EVEN WHEN IT'S HARD

Patience is a virtue. It's also something that you can build, just like any other muscle. Patience is about learning to be satisfied with the present moment and not letting yourself get caught up in what might happen in the future or how things used to be when they aren't anymore.

It's about being patient with yourself and others, especially if they're making life difficult for you right now!

Be proactive instead of reactive

Proactive is better. It's what you should be doing because it helps you to:

- Take control of your life. When things happen in the future, you can plan ahead for them and make decisions about how to handle them. You're in control of your own destiny, so don't let anyone tell you otherwise!

- Be more efficient. Being proactive means that when something does come up, instead of waiting until after it happens -which could be hours later or even days later- take action immediately before those things become issues on their own merits rather than just responding reactively.

Recognize how you're prioritizing your time

One good thing you can do is be honest with yourself. Are you spending your time on what matters most to you, or are you prioritizing other things?

To help answer this question, consider making a list of all your activities and rank them by importance. If something isn't getting done because it's low on your list, make changes so that it does fall higher up, or if nothing else works for now, just stick with what works!

If there are times when things aren't working out quite as expected or at all, don't be afraid to request help from others who know more about how life works than yourself: maybe someone has already made some similar mistakes themselves. You never can tell, there just might be other options available outside typical approaches like "just try harder" or "start over." It may seem like odd at first, but trust me, having someone else take responsibility for their part in this process will only make things easier in the long run and hopefully even fun.

Recognize what's wrong and what needs to change

The first step to solving a problem is recognizing it. Living in the present gives you a better chance of identifying what's wrong and what needs to change. Once you've identified the problem and its cause, it's time to plan how to solve it once and for all! This can be difficult because sometimes there aren't any easy solutions, but that doesn't mean there isn't anything we can do about our situations right now.

For example, if your job is causing stress, then maybe it's time for a career change. If you don't like your partner anymore, you may need counselling services or even divorce proceedings.

Think about what you really want out of life, and start making steps towards achieving those goals.

You know the first step to any goal is being clear about what you want to achieve. And, when you're clear on your goals, it's easier to make steps towards achieving them.

You may be thinking something like: "I want a better job. I want more money." Or maybe: "I want my kids in elementary school by this time next year." It doesn't matter how big or small these goals are; all that matters is that they're yours and not someone else's and are not focused on the past. Your focus should always be on where you are now -the present moment- and not worrying about anything else at all!

Break large projects into bite-sized tasks that you can deal with one at a time

Break large projects into bite-sized tasks that you can deal with one at a time. This helps you focus on one thing at a time rather than trying to do ten things at once. Once you've broken down the project into manageable chunks, put together a schedule for completing each task, and make sure it's not too difficult for you. Don't forget about tools like spreadsheets or calendars when planning out your workflow and deadlines. These help keep everything organized so that you know what needs doing and when in order to meet your goals and deadlines.

When making decisions or taking action based on what you want from life, don't let past experiences or opinions dictate how things turn out.

Don't sweat the small stuff

Living in the present is about being aware of what's going on around you, but it's also about staying focused on the big picture.

You'll find that if you take care of your mind and body, then things will fall into place naturally. When we worry about everything else but ourselves, we miss out on all the good things in life, which can make us feel stressed or upset when they're gone! Instead of sweating over small things -like what might happen tomorrow- focus on yourself instead. Eat well, exercise regularly, and promote positive thoughts throughout your day so that no matter what happens after dinner tonight, it won't ruin your mood for tomorrow morning.

Maintain a healthy sense of humour to help you get through difficulties

Humour is a great way to help you get through difficult situations. It can help you cope with depression, anxiety and other mental health issues by making them seem less serious or even funny. If you're feeling down, laugh at your own jokes to help lift your spirits and make light of things that might otherwise seem overwhelming.

If someone close to you is going through a hard time and needs support from friends and family members, provide emotional support but also humour as well! A quick joke will do wonders for everyone involved, especially if they're having an especially tough day themselves.

CONCLUSION

Conclusion

We hope that we've convinced you of the importance of living in the present. It is very easy to get caught up in your past and worry about the future, but taking a moment to stop and appreciate what's right in front of you is a great way to maintain balance and perspective. By focusing on what's happening right now rather than dwelling on old problems or hoping for things that may never come true, you'll feel more confident about moving forward with your life.

The tips provided are about living in the present, which we should all strive for. The future isn't guaranteed; it's something you have to work on every day. We're not saying it's easy, but by being proactive and thinking about what you want out of life, you can get closer to achieving those goals!

BONUS CHAPTER 2

SELF HEALING - HOW TO IDENTIFY AND GET RID OF EMOTIONAL PAIN

Self Healing

HOW TO IDENTIFY AND GET RID OF EMOTIONAL PAIN

INTRODUCTION

We've most likely all heard the phrase, "pain is a symptom, not the problem." The body's natural response to physical pain is to try to heal itself, so it can function as normally as possible. Sometimes this means the body needs time to recover or heal itself. Other times, though, get rid of your symptoms for good.

However, physical pain is not the only kind of pain there is. There is also something called emotional pain. Emotional pain can feel very real and very intense. But what is emotional pain, and how do you know if you're experiencing it?

If you're not sure whether your emotions are causing pain, there's no need to suffer alone. If you understand why your pain happens and take steps toward managing it effectively, you can get rid of your pain for good. In this chapter, we'll break down the signs that signal what your pain may be about and what steps to take next!

HOW TO IDENTIFY AND MANAGE EMOTIONAL PAIN

HOW TO IDENTIFY AND MANAGE EMOTIONAL PAIN

*E*motional pain is pain that originates from a non-physical source. It is a feeling that you feel inside of you -not necessarily your flesh- but your soul. It is mostly expressed in deep regret of, longing for, or need for something. It goes beyond sadness and is usually characterized by hopelessness, despair, and anger. Emotional pain can be caused by various factors, and it's not always easy to identify.

Emotional pain often occurs when something traumatic has happened or when there is some sort of change in your life. For example, if your partner suddenly leaves or gets sick and needs caregiving support, if you lose your job, or even if you move away from home for college and don't talk to friends anymore! However, the fact that someone may have experienced an event doesn't necessarily mean they will also experience emotional pain.

WHAT CAUSES EMOTIONAL PAIN?

Emotional pain is caused by a lot of things, the most common of which are loneliness, anxiety, and depression. Let's take a deeper look.

Loneliness

Loneliness is the feeling that you're alone in a world that seems to be full of people, and you feel like you have no one to talk to about your feelings. Loneliness can often make one feel like everything is out of control, leading to depression and anxiety.

It also makes one feel that nobody understands what one is going through. You may feel that nobody cares about your problems, or even worse, that they think the way you feel is wrong or simply not real. This can lead to feelings of shame, creating more emotional pain because it makes it difficult for you to reach out for help.

Regret

Emotional pain can be caused by regret for our past decisions; choices that seemed important at the time but didn't pan out quite how you had hoped they would when faced with them later on down the road. This can leave one feeling bitter, hopeless and cheated, thus leading to emotional pain.

Physical Events

Emotional pain can be caused by a traumatic experience like a death or divorce; it can also be caused by the loss or breakup of a relationship. A major life event such as losing your job may cause you to feel depressed or anxious for a while after this happens.

WHY DOES EMOTIONAL PAIN FEEL PHYSICAL?

It is not unusual to see people experiencing emotional pain that translates into physical pain. If you're experiencing emotional pain, it may feel like your body is suffering. You might have headaches, backaches, stomachaches, and even heartburn -all of which are signs that an illness has gotten to you.

If you have pain you can't explain, try looking into your emotions. Emotional pain is a common cause of unexplained physical symptoms. It's not a physical event that is literally damaging your body; instead, it's causing your brain to send signals of fear or anxiety through the nervous system into other parts of the body.

The mind and body are connected by an intricate network of nerve cells called neurons which transmit messages between them. When emotional stress or trauma causes the release of chemicals that interfere with this process, there may be changes in how nerve cells function and respond to signals from other parts of the brain. This could result in physical symptoms such as muscle tightness or cramps, headaches, nausea/vomiting or elevated heart rate/blood pressure.

How can you tell the difference between emotional and physical pain? To identify the difference between emotional and physical pain, it helps to understand what each one is.

Emotional pain can be caused by an event or feeling that you cannot control, such as being rejected by someone you love or having a childhood occurrence that still affects you today. This kind of emotional pain is often related to your thoughts, beliefs, and expectations about the world around you.

Physical pain is something that happens in your body or on its surface when there's damage being done. For example, when a tooth goes wrong because of decay, muscles contract too much during exercise, or nerve endings are damaged due to injury or disease.

How to Identify Your Own Emotional Pain

- Recognize the pattern.
- Take note of the frequency with which it occurs.

- Identify any triggers that make you feel this way.
- Look for changes in your mood that are caused by these emotions and try to identify why you're feeling them now instead of before or after them happening.

WAYS TO MANAGE EMOTIONAL PAIN

Talk to someone you trust

It can be quite hard to talk about your emotional pain, but it's important that you do. There are many people who want to help and support you in finding ways to manage your emotional pain. You need to find one and talk with them, be it a friend, family, or professional.

Try to understand the root cause of your pain

Asking yourself "why" is important in identifying what's causing your emotional distress and figuring out how best to handle it moving forward. A good place for beginning this process may be journaling or talking through what happened with a therapist.

Try some relaxation techniques

Relaxation techniques like meditation or yoga can help distract from negative thoughts while also helping calm body tension during stressful times or when you start to feel triggered.

When Should You Seek Help for Emotional Pain?

When you are experiencing emotional pain, it is important to seek help, as it is a sign that something is wrong.

When you're feeling emotionally hurt or sad, your body may feel tense or tight, and your muscles may have difficulty relaxing. You might have headaches or feel tired all the time as well. These symptoms can be signs of depression or anxiety disorders such as PTSD. Once you start having these physical symptoms, it is important for you to seek help for your pain. Rather than go visit a doctor at a hospital, these symptoms can be treated with counselling from licensed therapists who specialize in these issues and understand how they affect people's lives physically and mentally.

Rising Above Your Ego

Rising above your ego is a very important topic to discuss because self-healing cannot be complete without a change in mindset.

Your ego is an integral part of who you are and what makes you great. It's also a natural part of human nature, but it can sometimes get in the way of your success. When we're working towards something or trying to achieve a goal, our egos often get in our way because they want us to always be perfect. Our egos tell us that we have to do everything perfectly or else no one will like us or trust us, and this is never true! If someone doesn't like your work or if they don't trust what you're doing, then it's entirely possible that they just didn't understand the concept behind whatever project it was.

When I think of ego, I imagine someone who's too focused on themselves. Someone who thinks they're better than everyone else, or at least they deserve more than others. But the truth is that your ego can be a wonderful thing! The problem is when we let our egos get out of control when we allow ourselves to believe things about ourselves that are false and don't serve us well. If this sounds familiar, read on because I'm going to tell you how you can rise above your ego to live a happier life.

Here are a few important things you should know about controlling your ego:

Giving up your ego is not giving up your power

You're not giving up your power by giving up your ego. Ego is a tool for protection, and it can help you get ahead in the world. It's also a way of being seen, heard, and felt, which are all things that are important to all of us as humans. The best part? When we're not using our egos to protect ourselves from others, they serve as conduits through which we can positively connect with other people!

YOUR EGO CAN BLIND YOU

Your ego can also make you feel like you're always right, even when you are wrong. If someone disagrees with what you have said or done, it is easy for your ego to tell them that they are wrong and not being objective. This can be very frustrating for others who want to talk about something and get an honest answer from someone who doesn't have any kind of bias in the conversation.

Ego makes us feel like we're better than everyone else because it makes us think that we know everything there is to know about anything at all! The truth remains that there will always be people out there smarter than us -or more experienced in some areas. But if we spend time thinking about our own strengths instead of focusing too much on what others might lack, then maybe our egos won't blind us so often anymore!

Your ego is a big part of your social image

Your ego is a big part of your social image. It's what makes you feel good about yourself, what makes you want to be seen and heard, and what makes you feel like the best person in the room.

But it can also get in the way of your goals if not handled correctly. The key is knowing when to let go of this part of yourself in order for your true self -the one who cares about others- to shine through more often than not!

Taking care of yourself is not selfishness

Taking care of yourself is not selfishness. Selfishness is being self-centred, focused on your own needs and wants, without regard for the needs or wants of others.

Taking care of yourself does not mean you should neglect other people to do so. If anything, it means that you need to be mindful about how much time and energy you give to others vs how much energy and time goes towards taking care of yourself.

You can't always be everything to everyone, and that's okay

It's important to remember that you can't always be everything to everyone. You don't have to be perfect, but you also don't want to let yourself off the hook for not being perfect.

You're going to make mistakes, just like everyone else does. So instead of beating yourself up about how "bad" your mistakes were or how much money was wasted on them -which will only make things worse- think about what went wrong and learn from it so that next time something similar doesn't happen again.

So what do I mean when I say giving up your ego? Well, it's not giving up everything about yourself; rather than being defensive when someone criticizes something about you, try not taking it personally at all! Instead of getting upset about every little thing that goes wrong with their opinion/vision for how things should look/sound etc., think back on why those things might bother them so much, and perhaps try changing some aspects around until every-thing looks perfect again!

CONCLUSION

Conclusion

We hope this chapter has helped you to understand how to distinguish between emotional and physical pain. While it might not be possible to completely eliminate the former, it is important to know what causes it and how we can manage it in order to stay healthy.

We also hope this post has helped you identify your own ego, and we think it's important to take time to explore the parts of yourself that need improvement. We know it can be hard to let go of the parts of yourself you've built up to make sure you're safe and seen, but it's worth it. If you don't, you will be stuck in your ego and unable to see past yourself. The more you know about yourself, the better equipped you are for life outside of yourself.

It can seem like there are a lot of bad things about us, but really, there are good ones too. We all need some work on our egos and how we relate to ourselves. Hopefully, by putting some thought into these issues, you'll be able to develop a more balanced approach toward life and others around you.

Printed in Poland
by Amazon Fulfillment
Poland Sp. z o.o., Wrocław

31188563R00054